First published in Belgium and Holland by Clavis Uitgeverij, Hasselt – Amsterdam, 2015
Copyright © 2015, Clavis Uitgeverij

English translation from the Dutch by Clavis Publishing Inc. New York
Copyright © 2016 for the English language edition: Clavis Publishing Inc. New York

Visit us on the web at www.clavisbooks.com

Mack's World of Wonder. All About the Weather written and illustrated by Mack
Original title: *Wondere wereld. Meer over het weer*
Translated from the Dutch by Clavis Publishing

ISBN 978-1-60537-262-4

This book was printed in February 2016 at Publikum d.o.o., Slavka Rodica 6, Belgrade, Serbia

First Edition
10 9 8 7 6 5 4 3 2 1

Clavis Publishing supports the First Amendment and celebrates the right to read

WALL ABOUT THE WEATHER

Mack

Clavis

NEW YORK

WIND AND RAIN

CALM

When you're quiet, you can hear the sounds of nature. Can you hear the leaves rustling? That's the wind. Sometimes the wind blows really hard, sometimes it blows very softly, and every now and then it's so calm that you don't hear a thing. Branches stop moving, and there are no ripples in the water. When there isn't a breath of wind, lakes look as smooth as mirrors.

Hot air balloons float on the wind.
When there is no wind, the balloons go up
but they don't move forward. It looks funny!

Which weather vanes are pointing in the same direction?

LIGHT BREEZE

A gentle wind is also called a breeze. Animals and plants love it when there is a little bit of wind. A breath of wind blows flower seeds around. When the seeds land on a new spot on the ground, a lovely new flower grows. Little pinwheels love light breezes, too! They can't spin when there is no wind.

A glider can fly without a motor.
It floats on the wind.
Isn't that amazing?

Which grasses are blowing in the breeze?

STRONG WIND

When there is a strong wind outside, it's hard to walk. The wind hammers on you, and it can be hard to stand upright. When the wind is strong enough, it can even blow you around. You lean forward, and the wind just pushes you back. But be careful! The wind can also suddenly die down—and then you'll fall. *Bam!*

When there is a strong wind, clothes flap on laundry lines and can even blow away!

Who doesn't like the wind?

STORM

When the wind is so strong that you can hardly stay on your feet, you are in the middle of a storm. A storm usually announces itself well in advance. First the sky gets really dark, and then the rain starts to pour down. The wind gets stronger, too. Umbrellas and branches fly around. Pretty dangerous! When there is a storm, it's best to stay inside.

Umbrellas and branches
are flying around.

What is the storm blowing away?

SANDSTORM

There can be windstorms in the desert, too. The sand gets blown around and makes a huge cloud of dust. The cloud rages over the ground and covers everything in its path with a layer of sand. When people see the cloud approaching, they head for their houses. No one leaves their house during a sandstorm. Everyone stays safely inside, hoping that no sand will come through the chinks in the door!

Which animal is covered in sand?

HURRICANE

When there is a storm, there is a chance that your hat will fly off your head or that a branch from a tree will hit you. But a hurricane is much worse. A hurricane is a storm that's so strong, it can blow down a large tree in just a few seconds and sometimes even a row of trees. At sea, hurricanes make waves so high that even lighthouses can get swallowed by them. Hurricanes only appear in a few places on earth.

*A strong hurricane
can destroy a house.*

What did the hurricane break?

TORNADO

A tornado is a whirlwind. When there's a tornado, the wind starts spinning. Like a merry-go-round, it goes slowly at first, and then it goes faster and faster. You can actually see the wind whirling in a tornado. It looks a bit like a whirlpool in the air. Tornadoes suck up everything in their path—cars, houses, boats… everything! Tornadoes are like giant vacuum cleaners. Luckily, they don't occur often.

Which tornado is sucking up the most water from the sea?

FOG

Clouds usually float high up in the sky, but sometimes they come down and hang right above the ground. That kind of low-hanging cloud is called fog. A foggy landscape is very mysterious. It looks like a fairy tale! But it's not so much fun when you're driving a car or riding a bike. You can hardly see a thing. You always have to drive really slowly when there is fog.

In a dense fog, cows seem to be floating above the clouds!

Which animals are standing in the fog?

DEW

Early in the morning, when the sun has just come up and the grass is still a bit wet, you can sometimes see dew. The drops of water on the blades of grass are called dewdrops. You can find dew on grass and also on flowers, toadstools, and... cobwebs! Take a good look. It looks as if this spider's web is made out of tiny pearls. Those are dewdrops shining in the sun. Isn't it pretty?

Which flowers can you see dewdrops on?

DRIZZLE

Rain falls from the clouds in drops. But those raindrops aren't always the same size. When the drops are so tiny that you can hardly see them, it's called drizzle. Drizzle drops are so small, they are usually gone before they hit the ground. Sheep aren't afraid of rain and definitely not of drizzle. Because of its thick fur, this sheep hardly notices the mini-drops!

Birds can still fly when it drizzles.
But the drops are too big for the tiny wings
of butterflies and bees. Butterflies and bees prefer
to stay close to the ground.

Which drawing has run because of the drizzle?

SHOWER

You can get pretty wet from a rain shower. Big drops fall from a cloud, and puddles appear on the ground. Not everyone likes getting wet! You can hide from the rain underneath an umbrella, or you can step outside to feel the rain on your face and jump in the puddles with your rain boots!

If you see snails on the roads, it could mean it's going to rain.

Which elephant could use a rain shower?

DOWNPOUR

Some showers are very heavy. When it rains very hard, it's called a downpour. When you see big rain clouds approaching, you'd better take an umbrella because a rainstorm is coming! If you stand in a downpour with no umbrella for even a minute, you'll get soaking wet—just like a car at a car wash.

Smart animals take shelter during a downpour.

Which dog did not get caught in a downpour?

COLD
AND WARMTH

FROST

It can get really cold outside in winter—so cold that everyone wears a warm hat. When water freezes into little ice crystals, it's called frost. When frost forms on trees, they look as if they're covered in sugar. They can be very beautiful standing in a snow-white landscape with a deep blue sky above.

Which items of clothing keep you warm (and which one doesn't)?

ICE

When it freezes, water changes into ice. When it freezes hard enough, the ice will be thick enough to stand on. Or to skate on! Ditches, lakes, and rivers turn into ice-skating rinks. It's not easy to skate. The ice is slippery, and you'll definitely fall a few times when you first try it. But when you finally learn, you'll be able to glide across the ice, and it feels lovely! You can also spin and do pirouettes!

*Ice-skating is fun,
but it's pretty hard
at first!*

Which puddle hasn't frozen yet?

When it freezes, beautiful frost flowers can appear on the windows. They only grow on the inside. The cold from outside goes right through the glass and turns tiny droplets of water inside to ice. Then the drops of water next to them turn to ice, too. And so it goes on and on, until there is a beautiful ice-crystal picture on the window!

On the outside of the window, something beautiful appears when it freezes, too: icicles! The frost has turned this car into a giant ice statue!

What do you see under the icicles?

SNOW

When the weather is warm, rain falls from the clouds.
But when it's colder, the rain turns to snow. White snowflakes whirl
from the sky. Sometimes the snow melts immediately, but when it's cold
enough the snow remains and forms big piles. Birds don't like winter
weather; because of the cold snow, they can't find any food. You can help
birds in winter by building them a bird table.

You can build a nice snowman out of snow or make snowballs so you can have an exciting snowball fight.

Which animals are hiding in the snow?

HAIL

When it's cold, rain turns to snow. Or hail. Snow is light, soft, and fluffy, but hail is heavy and hard. Hailstones can be so small, you can hardly feel them. They can also grow into whoppers that are as big as tennis balls. If a hailstone that big fell on your head, it would hurt—a lot! As you can imagine, flowers and fruit really don't like hail. One hailstorm can ruin all the apples in an orchard. Hail can be dangerous!

It's almost always warm where meerkats live.
They've never seen such a crazy hailstorm!

Which flowers were hit by hail?

SNOWSTORM

Snowflakes usually whirl down quietly. But when it starts to snow really hard and a strong wind blows the flakes all around, you could find yourself in the middle of a blizzard. A snowstorm is beautiful to watch, but it's no fun to walk in. The cold snow hurts your face, and if you don't keep your coat tightly shut, you get all wet. Brrr!

Deer hate snowstorms. They can't see each other through the dense, raging snow. "Mommy Deer, where are you?"

Which sheep's nose is getting wet?

THAW

When it's not so cold outside, the ice in the ditch melts and the snow slowly disappears. There's a thaw! For swans and other water animals, a thaw is a party. The ice gets thinner and thinner and finally forms a puddle, where they can swim. The swans immediately start looking for food in the water. They are so hungry!

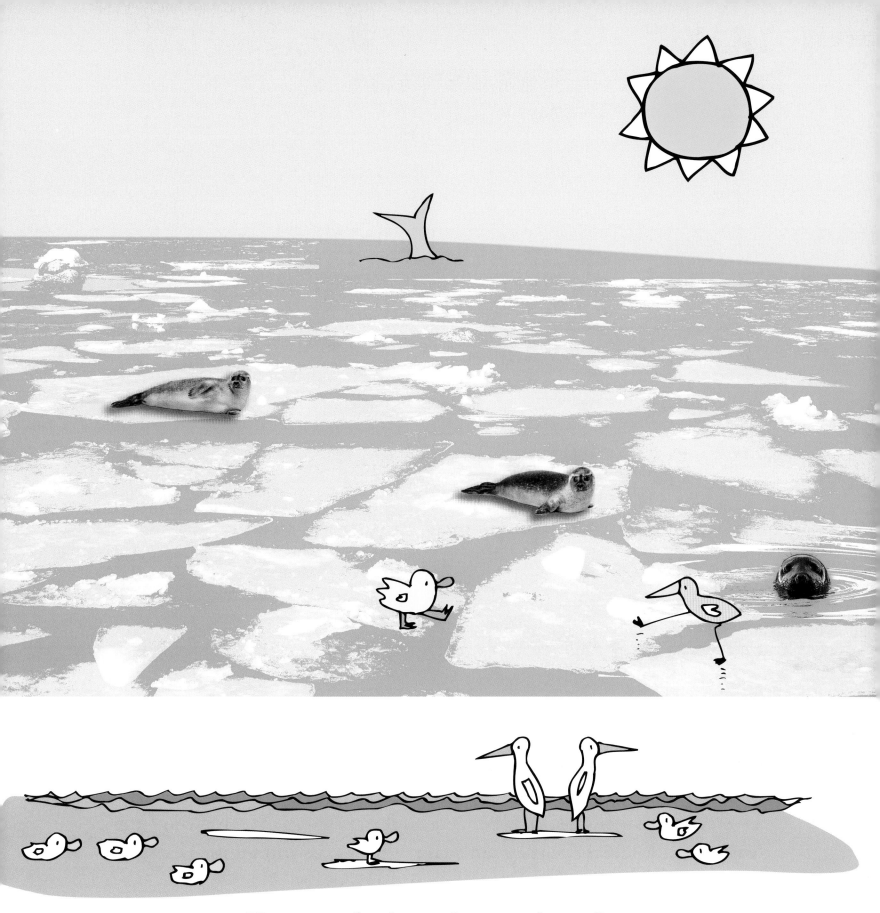

How many birds are there on the ice?

CHANGEABLE WEATHER

Dark clouds cover the sky. But look, the sun is breaking through! Is it going to rain? Or will it be a nice, sunny beach day? What do you think? The weather seems undecided! It keeps changing. Just when you make a beautiful sand castle, the rain could wash it away. And just as you're putting on your sweater, the sun starts to shine cheerfully. Changeable weather is exciting. You never know what's coming!

Birds fly through the rain,
and butterflies flit in the sun...
the weather is changing again!

Which animal likes the sun, and which one likes getting wet?

When the sun is high up in the sky, it can be nice and warm. Sweaters stay in the closet, and you can go outside. You could go to the beach or the playground, or you could play hide-and-seek in the garden. Most animals also like a little sunshine. Look—these birds are having a wonderful, cool bath. If you find it too hot in the sun, you can take a break in the shade.

Which bird is a little afraid of water?

HEAT WAVE

Phew, it can be boiling hot in summer. The clouds seem to have gone on vacation, and there is no wind. If it's really hot at least five days in a row, it's called a heat wave. During a heat wave, the sun shines so brightly that many people look for a cool spot. Some people stay under umbrellas, and others go swimming in the sea. This boy is about to jump into the water. *Splash!* It's so cool!

Which bear doesn't like the heat?

CLOUDS AND LIGHT

FLEECY CLOUDS

Clouds sometimes look like cotton balls floating in the sky. Clouds have different shapes and different colors, too. Some are big and gray and bring rain. Others are white and small, and the weather stays nice and dry. Some people call those white clouds "fleecy clouds" because they look a bit like the wool on a sheep. If you look closely, you can see things in the clouds: a knight with a sword, maybe a dragon? Clouds are so much fun!

Which animals do you see in the clouds?

THUNDERCLOUDS

Every now and then, the blue sky gets very dark—thunderclouds gather in the sky, and you'd better run inside quickly. Those threatening clouds don't look kind, and they aren't! A little while later, it starts to storm. It could rain or hail, thunder or lightning, sometimes all at once. Those thunderclouds aren't sweet, but they sure are exciting!

Which clouds are the thunderclouds?

EVENING GLOW

In the afternoon, the sun is no longer high up in the sky.
The sun sinks lower and lower and seems to be painting the sky.
The whole sky changes color. First the sky is bright blue, then it turns
yellow, then orange, and finally the sky turns deep red. The colors of
the clouds change, too, and the sky is beautiful! The colors only
disappear when the sun is completely gone and the dark night begins.

Which sun is really sinking?

POLAR LIGHTS

There are two places on earth where you can see the most spectacular light shows at night. The light of the sun seems to be dancing in the air. It changes color and shape. Sometimes it looks like a green curtain, and sometimes it looks as if enormous colored waves are rolling past. They could be white, orange, red, blue, or pink. This mysterious event can only be found in the cold upper and lower edges of earth: the North Pole and the South Pole.

Which sections of polar lights are exactly the same?

THUNDERSTORM

First you see a flash, and then you hear a deafening bang.
A thunderstorm is happening! It seems as if the clouds are very angry.
They make the sky dark and make more noise than a hundred lions. A flash
of lightning shoots out of those dark clouds and seeks the highest point
on earth. You should never stand under a tree during a thunderstorm,
because it's the highest point, and that's where the lightning will hit first.
Lightning flashes are very beautiful but also very dangerous. Be careful!

Which building is being struck by lightning?

RAINBOW

When the sun is directly behind you and it's raining in front of you, a beautiful rainbow can arc across the sky. Light is made of many different colors. It's hard to see the colors in the air, but the water droplets separate them and form rainbows, so you can sometimes see them when it's raining. Rainbows are red on the outside. Next comes orange, yellow, green, blue, indigo, and finally violet. Check and you'll see: the colors of the rainbow are always in that order.

You can also see
a rainbow in a waterfall.

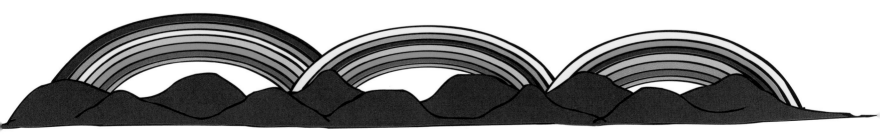

In which rainbow do the colors appear in the right order?

CLEAR NIGHT

At night, most people are asleep in their beds. But if you wake up in the middle of the night and look outside, you could see something very beautiful—that is, if there are no clouds. On a clear night, you can see thousands of stars in the sky. The stars sparkle like diamonds in the black sky. The longer you look, the more stars you will see. Go count them; you will soon be so tired that you'll go to sleep!

Which stars form the shape of a pan?

MORE ABOUT THE WEATHER

The weather makes beautiful works of art in nature.

This archway was not made by a sculptor, but by sand, water, and wind! If the wind blows on a stone for a very long time, it can blow away small bits. After thousands and thousands of years, the stone can look quite different. The weather makes many different kinds of art. When water freezes, beautiful icicles appear—sometimes even an entire ice castle!

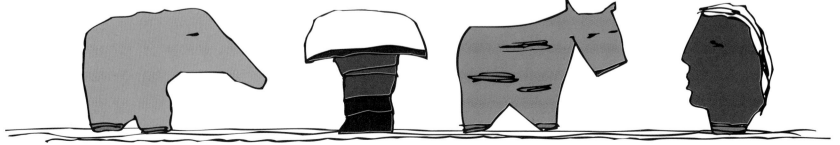

What shapes do these wind-worn rocks make?

THE WEATHER AND PLANTS

Plants need sunlight and water to grow, and the weather makes that possible. If there is no rain for a while, flowers hang their heads because they are thirsty. In fall, when it gets colder and the sun shines less often, the leaves on the trees change color until finally they fall off the branches. A few months later, in spring, when the weather gets warmer, new leaves grow on the trees, and the flowers come out again. The fields can look like large, multicolored carpets.

Which flowers could use a little rain?

Many animals don't need the weather report. They know exactly what the weather will be. An elephant knows that a thunderstorm is coming before it sees the first flash of lightning. That's because elephants feel the thunder from hundreds of miles away. Clever, aren't they? If a herd of elephants don't have enough water where they are, they'll run toward the thunderstorm. Where there is lightning, it will rain so hard that they will certainly be able to drink some water!

When swallows fly high,
the weather will be good.
When swallows fly low,
the weather will be bad.

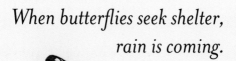

When butterflies seek shelter,
rain is coming.

When bees buzz,
the weather will be beautiful.

When roosters crow
in the afternoon,
it will rain soon.

Croaking frogs predict
beautiful weather.

Which bees are predicting beautiful weather?